Pete's Peculiar Pet S

The Wrong Jumper

Written by Sheila May Bird

Illustrated by Jim Field

Pete has a pet shop. It is not an ordinary pet shop. Oh no, Pete's pet shop has peculiar pets for sale. So it is called Pete's Peculiar Pet Shop.

There is Pete, feeding the pets. There is clumsy Mopsy, mopping the floor. And there is the bossy Griffin, telling her how to do it.

One day, when Pete was outside cleaning the fish tank, Mrs Muddyboot came into the shop. She had lost her glasses and was hunting for them in her handbag.

"Can I help you?" asked Mopsy.
"I hope so," said Mrs Muddyboot.
"I would like a jumper."
"I will see if we have one," said Mopsy.

She went outside to see Pete.

"Do we have any pets that **jump**?" asked Mopsy.

"No," said Pete. "But I will find one. Ask Mrs Muddyboot to return tomorrow."

Pete grabbed his bag of gadgets and went to look for a **jumping pet**.

In the park he met a man with a dog.
"My dog has fleas," grumbled the man.
"I'm sorry to hear that," said Pete.

Then Pete had a great idea.

"May I have one
of your dog's fleas?"
asked Pete.

"You can have
them all!"
said the man,
delighted.

10

Pete returned to the shop with the fleas. "I have a jumping pet for Mrs Muddyboot," he told Mopsy. "Tell her she can buy one and get the others free."

Mrs Muddyboot came into the shop while Pete was outside cleaning the slug pool.

"Have you found me a jumper?" she asked.

"Yes," said Mopsy. "It's a very small jumper."

"A small jumper is no good to me," said Mrs Muddyboot. "Please find me a bigger jumper. I'll return tomorrow."

So Pete went off to search for a bigger jumping pet. He found a very **jumpy frog** and took it back to the shop.

Mrs Muddyboot came into the shop while Pete was outside cleaning the Griffin's nest.

"Pete has found you a bigger jumper," said Mopsy. "It is in this box."

"A jumper that fits into that box is no good," said Mrs Muddyboot. "Please find me a bigger jumper."

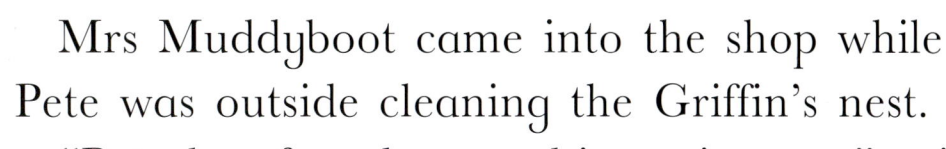

So Pete went to look for a bigger **jumping pet**.

At last, he found a kangaroo.

He took it back to the shop.

Mrs Muddyboot arrived while Pete was outside cleaning the windows.

"Pete has found you a really big jumper," said Mopsy. She went to get the kangaroo.

While Mrs Muddyboot waited, she looked for her glasses. This time she found them.

"Here you are," said Mopsy. "Jumpers don't get much bigger than this."

Mrs Muddyboot stared at the kangaroo. "I don't want a kangaroo," she said. "I want a jumper. A jumper to keep me warm!"

She gazed around the shop at the pets.

"Oh dear," she said. "There has been a mistake. This isn't the clothes shop."

"No," said Mopsy. "The clothes shop is next door."

The kangaroo and the frog smiled at Mrs Muddyboot. Although she couldn't see it, Mrs Muddyboot was sure that the fleas were smiling too.

"I will go next door to buy my jumper," said Mrs Muddyboot. "Then I will come back and buy the fleas, the frog and the kangaroo! I will take good care of them. After all …

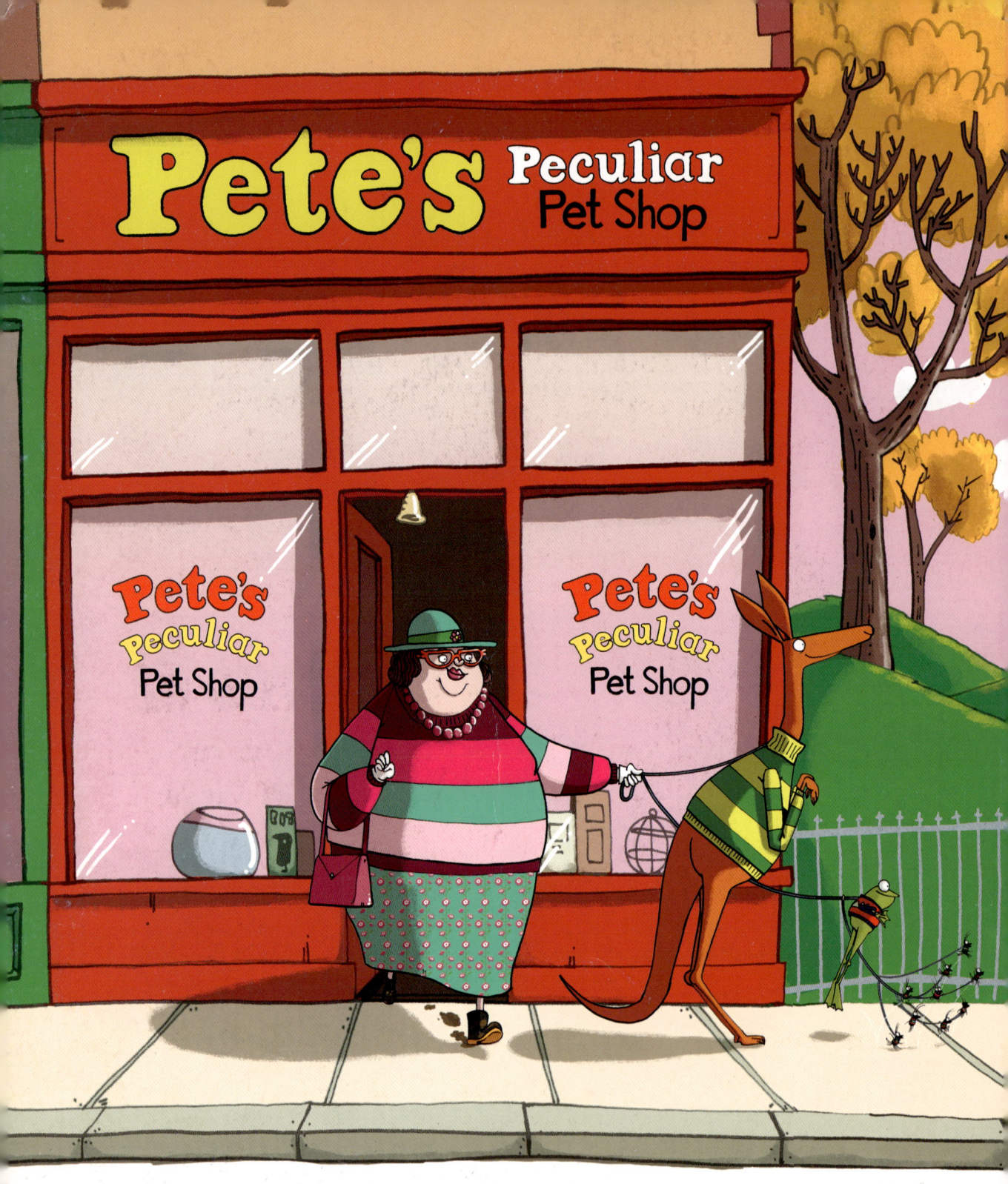

... you can't have too many *jumpers*!"